Portraits of Oxford

by Peter Coard

Kingsmead

Kingsmead Press
Rosewell House
Kingsmead Square
Bath

SBN 0906230 95 0

Text set in 11/13 pt V.I.P. Palatino, printed by photolithography
and bound in Great Britain at The Pitman Press, Bath

Contents

Peter Coard

The Radcliffe Observatory

Almost engulfed by Hospital buildings, this extraordinary edifice nevertheless deserves a close look. The original Infirmary like the Observatory was endowed by the Radcliffe Trustees, and survives, much altered, along the Woodstock Road frontage. It was finished two years before the Observatory was started by Henry Keene in 1772. Keene however died in 1776 and his design was considerably altered by his successor, James Wyatt. The tower, unexpectedly domeless for an observatory, has a version of the Tower of the Winds in Athens on top, complete with carved reliefs of the Winds with their Greek names. At a lower stage, and extending round the building are the signs of the Zodiac in patented Coade stone, almost as crisp now as when they were made two centuries ago. Some may be seen from the Infirmary car park from where this drawing was made, others are on the great bowed front at the rear.

PeterCoard

St. John's College

Originally founded as the Cistercian St. Bernard's College in 1437, and dissolved at the Reformation; the College was refounded in 1555 by a London merchant. The Front Quad is basically mediaeval, the style being continued into the Library in the south range of the Canterbury Quad at the close of the sixteenth century. However Archbishop Laud, a former President, completed the Quad in 1631–36 in a very different manner, particularly in the renaissance treatment of the loggia and magnificent central features, one of the latter being shown here. Exuberant carving surrounds le Seuer's statue of Charles I on this side of the Quad, whilst opposite there is a similar portal bearing his Queen, Henrietta Maria.

Peter Coard

Vanbrugh House

This curious monumental façade to what is now solicitors' offices can be found in St. Michael's Street – formerly known as New Inn Hall Lane. It is a reminder that Blenheim Palace is not so far away at Woodstock; and that whoever remodelled an earlier seventeenth century house here must have had some connection with Vanburgh and Hawksmoor. It seems probable that a family of craftsmen named Peisley were responsible. They are certainly known to have resided in St. Michael's Parish during the first quarter of the eighteenth century, and to have worked at Blenheim.

SPEEDWELL
CLEANERS
SPEEDWELL
CLEANERS
Peter Coard

Ship Street

Opposite the eleventh century tower of St. Michael's Church is this sympathetically restored timber framed building. There is a group of mediaeval buildings here, since the adjacent premises in Cornmarket Street are similar, although unrestored; and behind is a stone house before one reaches the rather heavy early twentieth century additions to Jesus College.

At the end of the pleasant row on the left, which backs on to the line of the former city wall is Turl Street. The prominent flêche is that of Exeter College Chapel. It was based by Sir Gilbert Scott on La Sainte Chapelle, Paris, in the mid-nineteenth century.

Peter Coard

Turl Street

Far from being 'the least attractive of the old parts of Oxford' as one writer has claimed, the Turl has much to offer the observer. It runs at first between the fronts of Exeter and Jesus Colleges, both refaced in Gothic style in the nineteenth century. Then follows Lincoln College where a small mediaeval window (to the left of the gatehouse) was recently discovered. Opposite is an attractive row of shops, mostly in timber framed houses. Even the modern buildings at the corner of Market Street do not impair the scene as their scale is right.

At the far end, facing the ancient Mitre Hotel is the former church of St. Martin and All Saints now beautifully restored as Lincoln College Library. This interesting building is reputed to have been designed by the 'amateur' architect Henry Aldrich, then Dean of Christ Church, who died in 1710. The spire, rebuilt in 1874, may be based on an unexecuted design in sixteenth century Rome. It is a dramatic accent in the unique skyline of Oxford.

Peter Coard

Radcliffe Square

The gentle curve of Brasenose Lane leads from the Turl, between Exeter and Lincoln Colleges past overhanging trees and the side of Brasenose College. Then comes a dramatic surprise – Radcliffe Square – one of this country's great urban spaces. Only a glimpse is shown here with part of Gibbs' Radcliffe Camera, and Hawksmoor's Codrington library for All Souls College.

But this is by no means all. As one walks on and around, the scene unfolds in all its varied interest: the south range of the Schools Quad (Bodleian library), Hertford College, more of All Souls College and the superb mediaeval University church of St. Mary the Virgin. Even more is to follow for across the grass and cobbles are the chapel of Brasenose College and the gatehouse which is illustrated overleaf.

Peter Coard

Brasenose College

The gatetower of 1512 is remarkable for its panelled front, very much of a contrast to the Radcliffe Camera. Indeed early in the eighteenth century there were plans by Hawksmoor for a rebuilding of the College in the 'grand manner', but these came to naught. Instead we are left with a most interesting and varied sequence of buildings, including a mid-seventeenth century chapel with unusual windows and a notable plaster fan vault. There is also now some exciting modern building of three centuries later tucked away behind the former church of All Saints.

The curious name of the College comes from Brasenose Hall, which was at one time on the site. The original mediaeval brass knocker (brazen nose) is now mounted in the place of honour above the High Table in the Hall.

Peter Coard

All Souls College

The entrance from the High' leads into the fifteenth century Front Quad. Through a narrow vaulted passage on the far right hand side is the larger North Quad, an architectural fantasy on the grand scale by Hawksmoor. Facing the side of the mediaeval chapel is the Codrington library, 'gothick' outside but classical within. This is adorned by a sundial made originally for the Front Quad and likely to have been designed by Wren when he was Bursar here in 1658. To the west are the colonnade, gatehouse and screenwall backing on to Radcliffe Square, whilst on the east are the twin towers illustrated here with the Common Room between them.

All Souls College has no undergraduates, only Fellows. It was due to the generosity of four former Fellows that the massive expansion of the eighteenth century took place.

ALFRED MARKS BUREAU
Peter Coard

126, High Street

There is so much of interest in the High' that a single building, and domestic at that, may well escape notice. However this example is remarkable for its elaborate treatment. It is a late seventeenth century remodelling of a timber framed house of the fifteenth century. Parts of the mediaeval barge board can be seen in the gable, whilst inside are said to be substantial traces of the line of the original frontage which was set farther back. The passage at the side is also a mediaeval feature. Other passages off the High' also lead to important survivals behind the existing façades. One of these is the seventeenth century Kemp Hall which is on the same side, nearer Carfax.

The Golden Cross
Ye Olde Coaching Inn
Peter Coard

The Golden Cross

An Inn since about 1200, the Golden Cross is entered through a fifteenth century archway at the Carfax end of Cornmarket Street. That is all that shows there, but inside is the uncommon feature of a long narrow cobbled courtyard. There are three ranges, which as can be seen are all different. Although greatly altered, the earliest is on the north side where the original fifteenth century oriel windows still project above later extensions. Opposite is distinguished late seventeenth century work, whilst at the far end is a range rebuilt in the nineteenth century.

PeterCoard

Tom Tower

Each night 'Great Tom', the bell from Osney Abbey, tolls one hundred and one times to commemorate the original number of scholars. Wolsey's foundation, 'Cardinall College' was intended to rival Kings' in Cambridge in size and magnificence. But Wolsey fell from power; and by 1546 his College and the Cathedral formerly at Osney were united as Christ Church.

It was left to Wren in 1681–82 to complete the unfinished gatehouse tower to Wolsey's enormous Quad in a deliberately 'gothic' style to 'agree with the Founder's work.' Since then there have been many additions to the College: Peckwater', the New Library, and Canterbury Quad, the ponderous Meadow Building of the mid-nineteenth century and the modern Blue Boar Quad. The resulting complex of styles is unique to the largest College in the University.

Peter Coard

Christ Church Cathedral –
The North Transept

Although one of the smallest of English Cathedrals, Christ Church is one of the most interesting. The chief glory is the intricate lierne vault to the Presbytery – a development from that in the Divinity School, and likely to be by the same master mason William Orchard who was buried here in 1504. Below is late twelfth century arcading, most unusual in the way that the triforium stage is enclosed. This in turn means that the aisles have their own arches below, complete with curious half capitals. This rhythmic design was continued round the church, appearing in the north transept which is shown here.

Before reconstitution by Henry VIII as the chapel of the College jointly with the seat of the new diocese, Christ Church was one of the very many religious foundations scattered in or around the city. Other parts of the former Augustinian Priory survive, and these also amply repay a visit.

PETER COARD

St. Frideswide's Shrine — Christ Church

The fragments of St. Frideswide's Shrine were discovered towards the end of the nineteenth century in a well at the west end of the Cathedral. They were then painstakingly reassembled and reerected in the form we see them now at the south side of the Lady Chapel, near to their original position.

St. Frideswide (Fritheswith – Bond of Peace) is said to have founded a nunnery here sometime in the eighth century. In course of time her remains became so venerated that at the end of the thirteenth century this shrine with its delicate naturalistic carving was constructed. The curious watching-loft nearby is rather later but is indicative of the importance in which she was held. After the vicissitudes which befell the former priory she came to be regarded not only as the patron saint of the University and City of Oxford but also of the new Cathedral and Diocese.

Peter Coard.

Oriel Square

The irregular urban scene is enlivened by the brightly painted range along one side and by this extraordinary curved wall and gateway which is actually at the back of the Peckwater Quad. Despite its seventeenth century 'mannerist' flavour it appears to have been erected sometime in the late eighteen-seventies. It makes a good contrast to Wyatt's quietly monumental entry to the Canterbury Quad and to the gables and gatehouse of Oriel College.

The name 'Oriel' derives not from the fine early seventeenth century oriel window over the entrance to the College but from an early house, 'La Oriole', which formerly stood on part of the site. This was Crown property and was acquired by the College in 1329 shortly after its foundation.

PeterCoard

Merton College — archway

Merton College has the distinction of being amongst the earliest foundations, 1264, of any of the colleges. Although the Hall was largely rebuilt in 1872–74 by Scott, the eastern arm of the outstanding chapel remains from this early period. Originally intended to be cruciform, only the choir, transepts, and tower were built, fortuitously setting the T-shaped precedent for so many other college chapels.

The view shown is of an early sixteenth century archway connecting the Hall with the Chapel sacristy. Buildings on the right are the backs of part of the early seventeenth century Fellows' Quad which boasts a four tier frontispiece. The entry to the left leads to the fourteenth century Mob Quad notable as being the earliest complete Quad in Oxford.

Peter Coard

St. Alban Hall — Merton Street doorway

St. Alban Hall, founded early in the thirteenth century was one of the many 'hostels' rented for students, the Masters teaching them on the premises. In mediaeval times there were very many more of these institutions than there were colleges. Gradually over the years they were replaced or absorbed by the colleges, St. Edmund Hall being the last survivor (1957).

St. Alban Hall was formally united with Merton College in 1881 after which it was mostly rebuilt and enlarged. However this entrance survives from an earlier rebuilding, the achievement of arms above the doorway being that of Benedict Barnham who left a legacy for that purpose in 1599.

Peter Coard

Magpie Lane

So named because of a former Inn, but previously known as Grope Lane, the little street narrows to a mere passage as it nears the High' opposite the church of St. Mary the Virgin. On the corner facing part of University College is a house now altered to make a Bank. The date 1588 can be seen incised on one of the projecting beams. The other houses on this side are also timber framed and are basically seventeenth century with later improvements.

Behind the point from which this view was taken is Kybald Street where can be found the former Parsons' Almshouses of 1816. Facing them is the interesting sequence of an ancient stone house cheek by jowl with a modern block, part of Corpus Christi College.

Peter Coard

The Queen's College — gatehouse

Nothing survives from the mediaeval buildings of the College founded by Queen Philippa's chaplain in 1340 as a rival to Edward the Third's King's Hall in Cambridge. [The latter became Trinity College in that City.]

In the sixteen-seventies a complete rebuilding in classical style was determined on, work probably commencing in the North Quad in the block facing Queen's Lane. Some part in the supervision of the works, if not the actual original design, was made by Wren. The layout of the Hall and Chapel range between the two Quads continues his concept but the detailing of this range and the remainder of the Front Quad is noticeably more baroque in character than would be expected of Wren. This applies particularly to the impressive screen wall and gatehouse which were designed by Hawksmoor and erected in 1734. Under the spectacular open rotunda is a statue of Queen Caroline, by Henry Cheere.

Peter Coard

Magdalen College Tower

Oxford owes its position to the confluence of the rivers Thames (Isis) and Cherwell, and it is remarkable just how many tributaries run through the city. It was on the banks of the Cherwell, outside the city walls, that Magdalen College was founded in 1458 by Bishop Waynflete, the then Bishop of Winchester. The site chosen included the former St. John's Hospital, a little of which still survives to the west of the tower. Building proceeded quickly, the tower, such a notable feature as one enters the city from the east, being begun in 1492. It was finished about 1509, and since about then it has been the custom to sing carols from the top of the tower each May Day at sunrise.

The Bridge, part of the abutment of which can be seen in the drawing, was erected in 1772–82 to the designs of John Gwynn of Shrewsbury. It was widened a hundred years later.

TURF TAVERN
MORNING COFFEE
LUNCH
BUFFET
DINNER
Peter Coard

Bath Place

Holywell Street, which has preserved its character to a remarkable degree, has retained many houses of the seventeenth and eighteenth centuries. It also has the University Music Room, which was opened in 1748 as the first building of its kind in Europe. It is still in use.

Immediately opposite its rather gaunt façade is the picturesque enclave of Bath Place which lies across the line of the city ditch. Behind the old houses which were remodelled in the eighteenth century is Hell (i.e. St. Helen's) Passage and beyond this can be seen part of the city wall. The line of the wall is represented to the west by the small octagonal chapel now incorporated in Hertford College. It occupies the site of a bastion and was built in the sixteenth century. Much more of the wall, with its bastions, can be seen to advantage in the grounds of New College. From this direction these may be reached through the late Victorian range a little way to the east along the street.

Peter Coard

New College – the Cloister

The College was founded by William of Wykeham in 1379 just before he founded Winchester College. It was the beginning of a new concept, that Fellows and students together should make up the college. Accordingly Hall, Chapel, Library, and sets were built together on a site in the northeast corner of the walled city. The cloister, which was consecrated in 1400 was apparently an afterthought for it is just off the axis of the main buildings; it is unlike other Oxford cloisters in standing apart from them.

The chapel, with its many treasures lies behind the point from which this view was taken, which is looking towards the tower of the Bodleian Library. Inside the cloister one can look up to the very fine pointed wagon roof; outside, the ancient stonework is set off to perfection by the magnificent specimen ilex.

Peter Coard

The Divinity School Vault

The Divinity School was begun in 1423, apparently the complex lierne vault not being originally envisaged. It antedates the vault in Christ Church by a few years and was completed about 1483.

'Duke Humphrey', the library above, commemorates Humphrey, Duke of Gloucester who was a notable benefactor. His Library was dispersed at the Reformation but a larger Library was opened in 1602 by Sir Thomas Bodley. The ensuing weight has on occasion affected the stability of the vault below; Wren being amongst those called in. To him can probably be ascribed the north doorway inserted in 1669; a few years after the House of Commons, taking refuge from the Plague in London, sat here.

FRONT COVER
The Sheldonian Theatre and the Clarendon building.

The exteriors of Wren's Sheldonian Theatre and Hawksmoor's Clarendon Building contrast greatly in their treatment of wall surfaces. Whilst Wren's work of 1664–67 has applied classical detail, Hawksmoor's is an uncompromising investigation in depth. Nevertheless Wren's work was revolutionary in being his first major work and in a style then new to Oxford. It was also daring in the design of the very wide roof trusses. These were necessitated by the dual nature of the Sheldonian' as first conceived. It was both a ceremonial theatre for the University, hence the Roman style painted ceiling; and the site of the University Press which perforce had to print in the basement, books being stored in the roof space.

The two concurrent uses can never have been entirely satisfactory for in 1712–15 the Clarendon Building was erected to house the Press. The detailing, particularly of the central ironwork, is outstanding; as are the lead statues representing the Muses to the designs of Sir James Thornhill. Two of these have been replaced recently.